PictureMaths

Year
3

Caroline Clissold

RISING★STARS

How to use Picture Maths

The objective of the *Picture Maths* series is to engage children in mathematics through pictures, interesting contexts and puzzles.

Each activity is spread over two pages of the book. The first page offers guidance on how the activity can be introduced, supported and extended. The second is a photocopiable page which provides an image that is the focus of the activity. There are questions related to a mathematics objective that are answered using information in the picture.

For each activity the guidance page includes a whole class introduction that can provide informal assessment about children's prior learning and introduces children to the picture. There are suggestions for how teachers can support children during the activities that are on the picture page and opportunities to extend children further, either to stretch their understanding or just because they are enjoying the context of the problem and want to dig deeper into the mathematics.

Being introduced to the context of the mathematical activities through pictures and discussion gives children the confidence to start the problem, supporting children with lower levels of English or reading. Children are required to use a variety of thinking skills and problem solving approaches, and there are lots of opportunities for them to talk about their mathematics and use mathematical language. Encourage children to ask questions about the contexts and the problems, then step back to allow space for independent work.

There is an activity for every area of primary mathematics, each carefully written to match the age group of the book. Many of the pictures form stories or links to other curriculum subjects that could be the basis of a longer project. The answers to all the problems are given in a solutions box on the guidance pages. All *Picture Maths* units and images are available to view and download on the CD-ROM, along with electronic versions of the extra mathematics classroom resources.

Measurement with Reasoning

Year 1	Year 2	Year 3	Year 4	Year 5	Year 6
		COMPARING AND ESTIMATING			
compare, describe and solve practical problems for: * lengths and heights [e.g. long/short, longer/shorter, tall/short, double/half] * mass/weight [e.g. heavy/light, heavier than, lighter than] * capacity and volume [e.g. full/empty, more than, less than, half, half full, quarter] * time [e.g. quicker, slower, earlier, later]	compare and order lengths, mass, volume/capacity and record the results using >, < and =		estimate, compare and calculate different measures, including money in pounds and pence (also included in Measuring)	calculate and compare the area of squares and rectangles including using standard units, square centimetres (cm^2) and square metres (m^2) and estimate the area of irregular shapes (also included in measuring) estimate volume (e.g. using 1 cm^3 blocks to build cubes and cuboids) and capacity (e.g. using water)	calculate, estimate and compare volume of cubes and cuboids using standard units, including centimetre cubed (cm^3) and cubic metres (m^3), and extending to other units such as mm^3 and km^3.
Top tips How do you know that this (object) is heavier / longer / taller than this one? Explain how you know.	**Top tips** Put these measurements in order starting with the smallest. 75 grammes 85 grammes 100 grammes Explain your thinking **Position the symbols** Place the correct symbol between the measurements > or < 36cm ☐ 63cm	**Top Tips** Put these measurements in order starting with the largest. Half a litre Quarter of a litre 300 ml Explain your thinking **Position the symbols** Place the correct symbol between the measurements > or <	**Top Tips** Put these amounts in order starting with the largest. Half of three litres Quarter of two litres 300 ml Explain your thinking **Position the symbols** Place the correct symbols between the measurements > or <	**Top Tips** Put these amounts in order starting with the largest. 130000cm² 1.2 m² 13 m² Explain your thinking	**Top Tips** Put these amounts in order starting with the largest. 100 cm³ 1000000 mm³ 1 m³ Explain your thinking

Measurement with Reasoning

Objective	Reasoning prompts
sequence events in chronological order using language [e.g. before and after, next, first, today, yesterday, tomorrow, morning, afternoon and evening]	**Explain thinking** Ask pupils to reason and make statements about to the order of daily routines in school e.g. daily timetable e.g. we go to PE **after** we go to lunch. Is this true or false? **Undoing** The film finishes two hours after it starts. It finishes at 4.30. What time did it start? Draw the clock at the start and the finish of the film.
compare and sequence intervals of time	130ml ▮ 103ml Explain your thinking 306cm ▮ Half a metre 930 ml ▮ 1 litre Explain your thinking £23.61 2326p 2623p Explain your thinking
compare durations of events, for example to calculate the time taken by particular events or tasks	**Undoing** A programme lasting 45 minutes finishes at 5.20. At what time did it start? Draw the clock at the start and finish time. **Undoing** Imran's swimming lesson lasts 50 mins and it takes 15 mins to change and get ready for the lesson. What time does Imran need to arrive if his lesson finishes at 6.15pm? **Undoing** A school play ends at 6.45pm. The play lasted 2 hours and 35 minutes. What time did it start?
estimate and read time with increasing accuracy to the nearest minute; record and compare time in terms of seconds, minutes, hours and o'clock; use vocabulary such as a.m./p.m., morning, afternoon, noon and midnight (appears also in Telling the Time)	**Undoing** A film lasting 200 minutes finished at 17:45. At what time did it start?

Measurement with Reasoning

MEASURING and CALCULATING

Objective	Objective	Objective	Objective	Objective	Objective
measure and begin to record the following: * **lengths and heights** * **mass/weight** * **capacity and volume** * **time** (hours, minutes, seconds)	choose and use appropriate standard units to estimate and measure **length/height** in any direction (m/cm); **mass** (kg/g); **temperature** (°C); **capacity** (litres/ml) to the nearest appropriate unit, using rulers, scales, thermometers and measuring vessels	measure, compare, add and subtract: **lengths** (m/cm/mm); **mass** (kg/g); **volume/capacity** (l/ml)	estimate, compare and calculate **different measures**, including **money in pounds and pence** (appears also in Comparing)	use all four operations to solve problems involving measure (e.g. **length, mass, volume, money**) using decimal notation including scaling.	solve problems involving the calculation and conversion of **units of measure**, using decimal notation up to three decimal places where appropriate (appears also in Converting)
Explain thinking What do we do before break time? etc.	**Explain thinking** The time is 3:15pm. Kate says that in two hours she will be at her football game which starts at 4:15. Is Kate right? Explain why.	**Explain thinking** Salha says that 100 minutes is the same as 1 hour. Is Salha right? Explain why.	**Explain thinking** The time is 10:35 am. Jack says that the time is closer to 11:00am than to 10:00am. Is Jack right? Explain why.	**Other possibilities** (links with geometry, shape and space) A cuboid is made up of 36 smaller cubes.  If the cuboid has the length of two of its sides the same what could the dimensions be? Convince me	**Other possibilities** (links with geometry, shape and space) A cuboid has a volume between 200 and 250 cm cubed. Each edge is at least 4cm long. List four possibilities for the dimensions of the cuboid..
Application (Can be practical) Which two pieces of string are the same length as this book?	**Application** (Practical) Draw two lines whose lengths differ by 4cm.	**Write more statements** (You may choose to consider this practically) If there are 630ml of water in a jug. How much water do you need to add to end up with a litre of water? What if there was 450 ml	**Write more statements** One battery weighs the same as 60 paperclips; One pencil sharpener weighs the same as 20 paperclips. Write down some more things you know. How many pencil	**Write more statements** Mr Smith needs to fill buckets of water. A large bucket holds 6 litres and a small bucket holds 4 litres. If a jug holds 250 ml and a bottle holds 500 ml suggest some ways of using the jug and bottle to	**Write more statements** Chen, Megan and Sam have parcels. Megan's parcel weighs 1.2kg and Chen's parcel is 1500g and Sam's parcel is half the weight of Megan's parcel. Write down some other statements about the

National Centre for Excellence in the Teaching of Mathematics

Measurement with Reasoning

measure the **perimeter** of simple 2-D shapes	measure and calculate the **perimeter** of a rectilinear figure (including squares) in centimetres and metres	measure and calculate the **perimeter** of composite rectilinear shapes in centimetres and metres	recognise that shapes with the same areas can have different **perimeters** and vice versa
Testing conditions A square has sides of a whole number of centimetres. Which of the following measurements could represent its perimeter? 8cm 18cm 24cm 25cm	**Testing conditions** If the width of a rectangle is 3 metres less than the length and the perimeter is between 20 and 30 metres, what could the dimensions of the rectangle lobe? Convince me.	**Testing conditions** Shape A is a rectangle that is 4m long and 3m wide. Shape B is a square with sides 3m. The rectangles and squares are put together side by side to make a path which has perimeter between 20 and 30 m. For example Can you draw some other arrangements where the perimeter is between 20 and 30 metres?	**Testing conditions** A square has the perimeter of 12 cm. When 4 squares are put together, the perimeter of the new shape can be calculated. For example: What arrangements will give the maximum perimeter?

to start with? Make up some more questions like this	sharpeners weigh the same as a battery?	fill the buckets.	parcels. How much heavier is Megan's parcel than Chen's parcel?

recognise and use symbols for pounds (**£**) and pence (**p**); combine amounts to make a particular value	add and subtract amounts of **money** to give change, using both £ and p in practical contexts

recognise and know the value of different denominations of **coins and notes**

Contents

1. The Pirate's Treasure

Objectives

- Read and write numbers to at least 1000 in numerals and in words
- Recognise the place value of each digit in a 3-digit number (hundreds, tens, ones)

Resources

- Coloured counters
- Rulers to draw number lines

Introduction

- Ask children to tell you what they can see in the picture. Point out the treasures and ask them to identify them: diamonds, rings, necklaces, goblets and coins.

- Ask children to estimate the number of diamonds. Count them together. Invite them to change their estimates if they wish towards the end of the count. They compare their estimate with the total. Give children tens and ones partitioning cards and ask them to make the number. Ask them to show you the tens and to say it. Repeat this for the ones. They write the number sentence 20 + 1 = 21.

During the activity

1. Inform children that the pirate hopes to sell the treasures to make money and these are the amounts shown in his thought bubbles.

2. Discuss how best to find out how many of each different treasure the pirate has. Give pairs of children piles of coloured counters and ask them to count out the numbers of each treasure. Observe how they do this. Encourage them to group the amounts into piles of 10. Once they have done this they count the tens and add the ones left. Discuss how they could count the total items of treasure. Encourage them to group the ones into more tens. They then count the groups of 10 in tens (10, 20, 30, etc.), count the ones and then combine. If children have difficulty counting all the treasures, encourage them to colour each type and count them as a class.

3. Write the numbers of treasure on the board in a random order. Ask children to order these from smallest to largest on a number line that they draw from zero to 100.

Extension

1. Children work out the differences in the numbers of other treasures with the number of coins. Give them number lines to help if required. Then encourage them to make number sentences to show their answers, e.g. 36 − 14 = 22.

2. Ask children to work out the different totals for the coins and one other type of treasure and to write a number sentence for their answers, e.g. 36 + 14 = 50.

Solutions

1. £225, £250, £375, £400

2. £175

3. 104 (21 diamonds, 14 goblets, 10 necklaces, 23 rings, 36 coins)

Maths words

numerals, digits, place value, partition, hundreds, tens, ones, total, difference, estimate

4

The Pirate's Treasure

The greedy pirate has found a treasure chest. He hopes to sell the treasure to make money.

1. The pirate is hoping to make money. Order the amounts from the smallest to the greatest amount. Plot them on a number line.

2. What is the difference between the least and the most money?

3. How many treasures has the pirate got altogether? Show how you worked out your answer.

2. Miranda Mermaid

Objectives

- Compare and order numbers up to 1000
- Count in multiples of 2, 3, 4, 5, 8, 10, 50 and 100 from zero

Resources

- Rulers to draw number lines
- Pendulum (could be made from three interlocking cubes on a piece of string)

Introduction

- Ask children what they can see in the picture. Can they identify and describe the creatures?

- How many legs has each octopus? How could children find out the total number of legs? Agree that they can count in 5s eight times or in 8s five times. Ask children to write down the multiples of 8 to 80 and circle the one that shows the total number of legs. Repeat this for the fronds of seaweed counting in 10s, and then the shells counting in 3s.

- Establish that Miranda has to count all the sea creatures to find out if any are missing. Children discuss how to do this with a partner. Take feedback.

During the activity

1. Encourage children to show their workings and to record their findings as they work.

2. Using Miranda's list of creatures, children order the numbers from smallest to largest and then position them on a number line from zero to 30. Encourage them to position 15 first or to divide their line into intervals of 10 to help with positioning. Invite volunteers to share strategies for finding the total number of creatures seen, the number on the list and the difference.

3. Discuss an efficient way to count the striped fish instead of counting in ones. Suggest counting in multiples of 2, 3 or 4. Practise this. As you swing the pendulum from side to side, children count in 2s from zero to 20 and back to zero, then 3s from zero to 30 and 4s from zero to 40. Each time count back to zero. Ask children to count the striped fish in these multiples. Repeat for the spotty fish.

Extension

1. Children write down the numbers of sea creatures on Miranda's list. For each number they write down 10 other numbers that are multiples of these, e.g. 5: 10, 15, etc. Encourage them to use strategies such as doubling and multiplying by 10.

2. There are the same number of sea creatures in 14 other areas of the sea. Children work out how many creatures that would be in total, including Miranda's area. (Solution: 75 octopuses, 60 seahorses, 30 crabs, 360 spotty fish, 270 striped fish, 135 shells.) Encourage them to partition 15 into 10 and 5, find 10 lots of each number and 5 of the other, and then total them. They then order these numbers from smallest to largest.

Solutions

1. Octopuses 5, seahorses 4, crabs 2, spotty fish 16, striped fish 12, shells 9
2. 28
3. 42 fish; there are 28, so 14 are missing

Maths words

order, hundreds, tens, ones, multiple, count in 2s or 5s and so on

Miranda Mermaid

Miranda Mermaid is counting all the sea creatures that live near her. She wants to make sure none are missing.

I hope all my sea animals are here. It's very difficult to count them.

Miranda's sea creatures

Octopuses : 5
Seahorses : 4
Crabs : 2
Spotty fish : 24
Striped fish : 18
Shells : 9

1. How many of each sea creature can you count? Try to count them in 2s, 3s or 4s.

2. How many fish are there?

3. How many fish should there be? How many are missing?

3. The Special Mission

Objective

⊚ Accurately add numbers mentally including pairs of one- and 2-digit numbers, 3-digit numbers and ones, 3-digit numbers and tens, 3-digit numbers and hundreds

Resources

⊚ Tub of counters per pair of children

⊚ Rulers to draw number lines

⊚ Digit cards for extension activity

Introduction

⊚ Ask children to tell you what they can see in the picture and to describe what they think is happening. Perhaps the space ship is trying to save lots of animals whose habitats are in danger. It will take them to a new home.

⊚ Can children identify the animals? Discuss how best to find out how many animals will be on the space ship when they are all on board.

⊚ Ask children to estimate the number of animals walking towards the space ship. Discuss an efficient way to count them. Agree that, since there are pairs of animals, counting in 2s could be appropriate. Children count in 2s and then compare this with their estimate. Whose estimate was the closest? Focus on estimating and counting. Give pairs of children a tub of counters. They take several handfuls out of the tub and put them in a pile on the table. They estimate how many there are and then count in an efficient way which could be in 2s or grouping them in 5s or 10s.

During the activity

1. Ask children the numbers of animals that are already in the space ship. They draw a number line from zero to 100 and plot these numbers onto it. They rehearse finding differences by counting on from one number to another.

2. Discuss how they could find out how many animals will be on the space ship altogether. Agree that they could add all the different numbers together. Rehearse addition of 3-digit numbers by adding the most significant digits first.

3. Encourage children to show how they worked out their answers.

Extension

1. Children use digit cards to make three 3-digit numbers. They imagine that these are new numbers of animals and find their total.

2. Ask children to make up problems from the picture that can be answered using addition.

Maths words

add, addition, total, altogether, more, estimate

Solutions

1. 24

2. 48 + 32 = 80

3. 80 + 24 = 104

The Special Mission

This space ship is on a special mission to save the animals on Earth.

1. How many animals are on their way to the space ship?

2. How many animals are on the space ship already?

3. How many animals will be on the space ship when all of them are on board?

4. The Toy Shop

Objectives

- Subtract numbers with up to 3 digits, including using columnar subtraction
- Add and subtract amounts of money to give change, using both £ and p

Resources

- Rulers to draw number lines

Introduction

- Ask children to tell you what is happening in the picture and to identify the different toys.

- Rehearse some data-handling skills by asking children to vote for their favourite toy. Make a tally of their choices, then put these in a table. This could lead into making a bar graph or pictogram.

During the activity

1. Encourage children to keep their jottings and to write down their methods.

2. Ask children to order the prices of the toys from least to greatest, placing them on a number line from £0 to £100. Encourage them to place marker amounts (£50, £25, £75) on the line to help them position the amounts more accurately.

3. Can they tell you which is the most expensive toy? Can Cindy afford it? Why not? They work out how much more money she would need to buy it. Repeat this for the other toys that cost over £20. Can they tell you the cheapest toy and how much under Cindy's budget it is? Repeat this for other toys that are less than £20.

4. Ask children to suggest pairs of toys that Cindy can afford. Rehearse methods for addition, e.g. partitioning and adding the pounds first and then the pence, the extended written method, and the short written method if appropriate. Then children choose pairs of toys and find their totals. Encourage children to be systematic, e.g. they choose one toy and then add different pairings to it.

5. Model an example of finding differences between the costs of different pairs of toys using various strategies, e.g. count on from the cheapest to the most expensive, keep the first number whole, partition the second and take the parts away from the whole and the short written method if appropriate.

Extension

1. For the toys that children found in question 2, ask them to work out the total cost for each pair and the change that would be left from Cindy's £20.

2. Ask children to investigate how many groups of three different toys Cindy can buy for her money.

Maths words

add, addition, total, subtract, take away, difference

Solutions

1. Car £25, football set £25.50, skateboard £28.50, doll's house £36, keyboard £38, table football £50, racing car set £65.40

All other answers are according to children's choices.

The Toy Shop

Cindy has been given £20. She would like to buy two toys.

1. Write down the toys that Cindy can't buy because she doesn't have enough money.

2. Choose pairs of toys that you think Cindy can afford to buy. Work out their total costs.

3. Pick pairs of toys and work out the difference in price between them.

5. Party Time!

Objectives

⊚ Accurately subtract numbers mentally including pairs of one- and 2-digit numbers, 3-digit numbers and ones, 3-digit numbers and tens, 3-digit numbers and hundreds

⊚ Add and subtract amounts of money to give change, using both £ and p

Resources

⊚ None required

Introduction

⊚ Discuss what is happening in the picture. Establish that the twins are deciding which entertainment to have at their party. Which would children choose?

⊚ Volunteers tell the rest of the class about parties and what they did at them.

During the activity

1. Encourage children to use mental calculation strategies as much as they can.

2. Ask children how much *Magic!* charges. How much will it cost for 2 children? Invite volunteers to explain how they worked it out (solution: £7). Next ask children to work out the cost for 4, 8 and 16 children (solution: £14, £28, £56). Encourage children to use doubling strategies. Next ask for combinations (e.g. to find the cost for 12 children, add 4 and 8 children).

3. Ask children to tell you how many lots of 30 minutes there are in 1 hour and then 2 hours. Establish that there will be four lots. Discuss how they can work out the total cost of *Music4You*. Agree that they need four lots of £15. Encourage them to work this out by doubling through partitioning, for 1 hour, and then doubling again for 2 hours.

4. How many children will be at the party? Discuss ways of finding prices for 20 guests. Agree that they could add 20 times, but a simpler way might be to find 10 amounts and then double that amount or add twice. Put some prices on the board, e.g. 75p. Children find 10 lots by multiplying so that each digit moves to the left, the ten pences become pounds giving £7.50. They then add this twice using a partitioning strategy.

Extension

1. Children work out how much below or above budget the prices for the different entertainments are.

2. Ask children to work out how much each entertainment will cost for 40 children.

3. Take the opportunity to practise doubling numbers to 20 and finding multiples of 5 to 100.

Solutions

1. £60

2. £25, £50; £35, £70

3. They can't afford *Music4You* as this would cost £60 for 2 hours. They can only afford *Clowns R Us*.

Maths words

add, addition, total, subtract, take away, difference, how much more/less

Party Time!

Twins Sam and Sammy are having a birthday party. They have £50 to spend on entertainment.

1. How much does *Fun 'n Games* charge for two hours? Show how you worked this out.

2. How much will *Clowns R Us* charge for 10 children? Use your answer to work out how much it will cost for 20 children. Do the same for *Magic!*

3. Can the twins afford to have *Music4You* at their party? How do you know? Which entertainment can they afford?

6. Open the Safe!

Objective

◎ Solve missing number problems, using number facts, place value, and more complex addition and subtraction

---

Resources

◎ Counting stick

Introduction

◎ Ask children what they think the picture is about. It's a spy trying to open a safe to get some important papers. Why might he need the papers?

◎ Read the safe code instructions together.

During the activity

1. Remind children to show their jottings and workings, and to look carefully at the operations used.

2. What can children tell you about the first safe code? Discuss the operations used – addition and subtraction, and ways of finding the missing numbers, e.g. counting on from the given number to the answer or taking the given number from the answer. Write up some addition missing number sentences for children to solve, e.g. $36 + ? = 52$, $? + 48 = 124$ (solution: 16, 76). Repeat for subtraction missing number sentences, e.g. $36 - ? = 12$, $? - 14 = 28$ (solution: 24, 42). Discuss strategies, e.g. counting on from the answer to the first number or adding the answer to the second number.

3. Discuss finding digit totals – add the digits of a number together until they have just one digit.

4. Discuss the operations used in safe code 2 – multiplication and division. Use this opportunity to practise times tables facts and corresponding division facts using a counting stick, with zero at one end and 30 at the other end. What steps must children count in to get from one end to the other? Agree 3s. Count forwards and backwards in 3s. At different points stop, e.g. at 18, to ask children how many 3s make 18 and what they would divide 18 by to get 3.

5. Write some missing number sentences for multiplication and division, e.g. $4 \times ? = 36$, $28 \div ? = 4$ (solution 9, 7). Discuss strategies, e.g. counting on in steps of the smaller number to the larger to find how many are needed or using the inverse operation.

Extension

1. Children make up missing number clues to open a safe. They swop these with a partner to solve.

2. Ask children to make up numbers that will have a digit total of 6, 9 and 3.

Maths words
add, subtract, multiply, divide, missing number, inverse operation

Solutions

1. 8, 7, 17, 2. Total 34. Digit total 7.

2. 9, 6, 6, 4. Total 25. Digit total 7.

3. 5, 7, 3, 8. Total 23. Digit total 5. 775 opens the safe.

Open the Safe!

This spy is trying to open the safe. Inside are secret papers that could save the country!

1. Work out the missing numbers for safe code 1. Now add the missing numbers together. Then add all the digits together until you have just one digit. What number do you have?

2. Work out safe code 2 in the same way.

3. Now work out safe code 3. Which three numbers will open the safe?

7. Which Dog Food?

Objective

◎ Recall and use multiplication and division facts for the 2, 3, 4, 5, 8 and 10 multiplication tables

---

Resources

◎ Digit cards

Introduction

◎ Ask children to describe what is happening in the picture. Establish that Armani has £20 to spend on dog food and wants to buy as many tins as she can in a selection of flavours.

◎ Ask children to tell you how they could do this and what mathematics is involved. Agree on multiplication and addition.

During the activity

1. Remind children to use their times tables and to show their workings.

2. Discuss ways to work out how much it will cost to buy 6 of Yum's tripe & chicken dog food. Agree they could add each amount six times, but that using multiplication tables would be more efficient. Practise saying the 6 times table to 12 × 6, then ask how this can be used to work out the cost. Establish that they could change the tens number in the price to ones, multiply it by 6 and then make it a tens number again, e.g. tripe & chicken: 9 × 6 = 54, 90 × 6 = 540, total cost £5.40. Repeat for the other flavours on the bottom shelf.

3. Ask children to work out the total cost of buying 8 of each tin on the third shelf down. First practise finding 8 times table facts. Hold up digit cards, one at a time. Children multiply each number by 8. Invite volunteers to write on the board the appropriate number sentence and the corresponding division. Discuss how to find 8 of each flavour by multiplying the tens number by 8, e.g. chicken in jelly: 5 × 8 = 40, 50 × 8 = 400, total cost £4. Repeat this for other tables that children need to practise.

Extension

1. Children order all the different prices of dog food on the four shelves. They position these on a number line from £0 to £1. Encourage them to mark on helpful numbers so that they can position the others more accurately, e.g. 50p, 25p and 75p. Ask them to find differences between pairs of prices.

2. Children work out how many of each flavour Armani can afford to buy for £20. Encourage them to record their results clearly in a table.

3. Ask children to choose three flavours of dog food and to work out some of the possible combinations they could buy with £20, getting as close to £20 as possible.

Maths words
multiply, multiplication, double, divide, division

Solutions

1. £3.50

2. £1.60

3. Children's choices

Which Dog Food?

Armani is buying dog food. She wants to buy as many tins as possible for £20 and get different flavours.

1. How much will it cost to buy 5 tins of Yum's beef dog food?

2. How much will it cost to buy 4 tins of Scrum's tripe dog food?

3. Choose some tins of dog food for Armani to buy. How much will she spend?

8. Fred's Football Kit

Objective

⟳ Write and calculate mathematical statements for multiplication within the multiplication tables; and for 2-digit numbers × one-digit numbers, using mental and written methods

Resources

⟳ Pendulum (made from three interlocking cubes and a piece of string)

⟳ Rulers to draw number lines

Introduction

⟳ Establish that Fred is the manager of a football club and that he needs to buy new kit for 15 of his players. He wants to buy it in the shop that will give him the cheapest price.

⟳ Discuss how to find this out and the mathematics needed – multiplication and addition.

During the activity

1. Ask children to look at the prices of the shorts in all the shops. Agree that these are all single-digit numbers. Swing the pendulum. As it swings from side to side, children count in multiples of each of these numbers to the 12th multiple. Write up the finishing numbers. Ask children to count three more multiples onto each to find the cost of 15 pairs of shorts. Ask children to think of another way that they could find the cost of 15 pairs of shorts. Agree that they could partition

Solutions

1. *Fit4all* £105.00, cheapest *SportsRus* £60.00, *Time2play* £75.00, *Sports4me* £90.00.

2. *Sports4me* cheapest at £150, *SportsRus* most expensive at £210.

3. *Fit4all* £48, cheapest *SportsRus* £47, *Time2play* £51, *Sports4me* £49.

the 15 into 10 and 5 and multiply each of these by the price of shorts and then recombine the numbers, e.g. $10 \times £7 = £70$, $5 \times £7 = £35$, $£70 + £35 = £105$.

2. Ask children to order the prices of the shorts, shirts and boots from each shop on a number line from £0 to £40. Encourage them to plot £20, £10 and £30 first so that the numbers can be positioned more accurately. They could use this to work out differences in prices, e.g. between the cheapest and most expensive of each item.

3. Ask children to tell you the price of each shirt. Agree that these are 2-digit numbers. Discuss how to multiply these by 15. Establish that they could again partition 15 into 10 and 5 and multiply the prices by each number. Point out that, once they have multiplied the number by 10, they could halve it for multiplying by 5. This works because 5 is half of 10. Repeat for the boots.

Extension

1. Children work out how much it would cost to buy 15 sets of kit at each shop (solution: *Fit4all* £720, *SportsRus* £705, *Time2play* £765, *Sports4me* £735). First they add to find the total cost of one kit. Then they multiply by 15. Encourage them to multiply by 10, halve that for 5 and then total the two.

2. Can children think of a cheaper way that Fred could buy 15 sets of the kit? Establish that he could buy the cheapest item from each shop (solution: £630).

Maths words

multiply, multiplication, times, partition, double, halve

Fred's Football Kit

Fred is the manager of this football club. He needs to buy new kit for 15 footballers.

1. How much will 15 pairs of shorts cost Fred at each of the shops? Which is the cheapest shop for shorts?

2. Which is the cheapest shop for shirts? How much will it cost him to buy 15 shirts here? Show how you worked this out. Now do the same for the shop with the most expensive shirts.

3. Work out how much it will cost to kit one player at each shop. Which shop is the cheapest?

19

9. A Fishy Problem

Objective

🌀 Write and calculate mathematical statements for division within the multiplication tables; and for 2-digit numbers × one-digit numbers, using mental and written methods

Resources

🌀 Counters

🌀 Rulers to draw number lines

Introduction

🌀 Explain that Edward has had a delivery of goldfish. How many goldfish must Edward put in each bowl so that there are an equal number in each and none left in the tank? Discuss the mathematics they will need to work this out – division.

🌀 Ask children to tell you all they know about division, including vocabulary, e.g. share, divide, groups of. Establish that division is the inverse operation to multiplication and that they can often use multiplication to solve a division.

During the activity

1. Give each child 24 counters to represent the goldfish. Ask them to work out how many groups of 2 they can make. Agree that they can make 12 groups. Write up the number sentence 24 ÷ 2 = 12. Discuss the idea that children can check this by counting in 2s twelve times to see if they get to 24. Do this together. Encourage them to record this on paper by drawing 24 goldfish and drawing

loops around pairs. Do they end up with 12 groups?

2. Ask children to put their 24 counters into groups of 3, 4, 5, 6, 7, 8, 9 and 10. They record this using pictures. Then ask them to list those that divide out equally. Discuss the idea of the remainder being the number left over, e.g. 24 ÷ 5 = 4 remainder 4.

3. Encourage children to use these methods to work out the questions and record the answers.

Extension

1. Children work out all the possible numbers of bowls that Edward could use for his 24 goldfish so that there are the same number in each.

2. Give children higher numbers of goldfish to put into the 8 bowls with an equal number in each, e.g. 48. They could do this by counting on along a number line in different steps to see which will land on 48.

3. Practise dividing other 2-digit numbers below 40 by a single-digit number by pretending that Edward has different numbers of other pets delivered to his shop. Children use counters to group them and then record this using pictures or symbols and write the appropriate division number sentence. Finally they check their answers by counting up in steps of the divisor.

Solutions

1. 24 goldfish; 8 bowls

2. 8 goldfish left in the tank; 4 empty bowls

3. 3 goldfish in each bowl

Maths words

divide, division, groups of, divisor

A Fishy Problem

Edward owns a pet shop. He needs to put equal numbers of goldfish in the round bowls.

1. How many goldfish are there? Try to count them in 2s. How many round bowls are there? Count these in 2s too.

2. If Edward put two goldfish in each bowl, how many would be left in the tank? How many empty bowls would there be if he put 6 goldfish in each bowl?

3. Work out how many goldfish need to be in each bowl so that the bowls have the same number of goldfish and so that there are none left in the tank.

10. Sweeties!

Objective

🌀 Solve missing number problems, using number facts, place value, and more complex addition and subtraction

Resources

🌀 Counters

🌀 Extra photocopies of the picture for extension activity

Introduction

🌀 What can children tell you about the picture? Establish that the boys can choose 12 sweets each but can't decide how many of each to have.

🌀 Looking at the sweets on the table, can children describe this as an array?

During the activity

1. Can children tell you how they could use an array to work out the number of sweets? Agree that they could multiply 12 × 4 or 4 × 12. Ask them to do this. Write a missing number sentence on the board and ask them to use what they have just done to find the number, e.g. 12 × ? = 48, ? × 4 = 48, 48 ÷ ? = 12. Give pairs of children 48 counters and ask them to make up other arrays. Can they find them all, i.e. 1 × 48, 2 × 24, 3 × 16, 4 × 12, 6 × 8?

2. Write some missing number sentences on the board. These should have two, three or four numbers on one side of the equals sign and 12 on the other to represent Zabby's choice of sweets. Begin with two, e.g. 4 + ? = 12; then three, e.g. 2 + ? + 5 = 12; and finally four, e.g. ? + 4 + 3 + 1 = 12. Discuss the strategy, i.e. add those they know together and then count on to 12.

3. You could then make up some number sentences that have two missing numbers, e.g. ? + ? = 12, ? + 3 + ? = 12, 1 + ? + ? + 5 = 12. Children need to work out all the possible solutions to help them with the questions.

Extension

1. Children work out all the possible options for Zabby choosing two sweets, then three and finally four. They need to work systematically and make a table of their results.

2. Children make up different missing number sentences for the 48 sweets using addition and subtraction.

3. Children imagine that Yukesh has taken some sweets. Make up missing number sentences for subtraction, e.g. 48 − ? = 36, 48 − ? = 21. If they need support, they can cross out the answer on a photocopy of the picture and count how many are left. Discuss strategies such as counting on from how many are left to the original total.

Solutions

1. 48; counting in 4s or multiplying 4 by 12

2. 3 of each

3. Check children's answers.

Maths words
array, multiply, divide, total, equal

Sweeties!

Zabby and Yukesh are allowed to choose 12 sweets each.

1. How many sweets are on the table? How did you work that out? If you counted in ones, think of another way to count them.

2. Zabby picks an equal number of each type of sweet. How many of each will he have?

3. Draw five different combinations of sweets for Zabby to choose from. Write an addition number sentence for each.

11. Lovely Lights

Objectives

◎ Identify, name and write unit fractions up to $\frac{1}{12}$

◎ Compare and order unit fractions and fractions with the same denominators

Resources

◎ Strips of A4 paper about 2 cm wide

◎ Rulers

◎ Counters

Introduction

◎ Ask children what they think is happening in the picture. Ask volunteers to read what the children are saying. Discuss the properties of each shape and ask children about thirds.

◎ Recap the basics of fractions, e.g. the denominator shows how many a shape or number must be divided by and the numerator shows how many parts are needed, the higher the denominator the smaller the fraction.

During the activity

1. Remind children that the boy suggested buying a third of each type of lantern. Give each child a strip of paper to fold into three equal pieces, measuring with a ruler if they need to. They label each section '$\frac{1}{3}$'. Repeat this for sixths using another paper strip. Ask questions, e.g. how many thirds/sixths are the same as a whole? How many sixths are the same as $\frac{1}{3}$, $\frac{2}{3}$? Which is bigger $\frac{1}{3}$ or $\frac{2}{3}$, $\frac{1}{6}$ or $\frac{1}{3}$? How do they know?

2. Give pairs of children 30 counters. They work out which numbers from 3 to 30 can be shared equally into thirds, perhaps placing them onto their paper strip. Repeat for sixths. Which numbers can be shared into both? What do they notice about these numbers? (Solution: they are multiples of both 3 and 6.)

3. Ask children to draw lanterns like those in the picture, drawing numbers they know can be shared into thirds. They find out how many $\frac{1}{3}$ of each set of lanterns is.

4. Remind children to show how they work out each question.

Extension

1. Children explore other fractions, e.g. ninths, twelfths. They find numbers that can be divided equally into these fractions and draw lanterns to show their results.

2. Give children some numbers up to 100. They write number sentences to show into what amounts they can be shared equally. Begin with 24, i.e. $\frac{1}{2}$ = 12, $\frac{1}{3}$ = 8, $\frac{1}{4}$ = 6, $\frac{1}{6}$ = 4, $\frac{1}{3}$ = 8, $\frac{1}{12}$ = 2. Children then use their findings to order the fractions from smallest to largest.

Maths words

fraction, unit fraction, numerator, denominator

Solutions

1. 9, 3

2. 12, 4

3. 18, 6; buy 13

Lovely Lights

These friends are choosing party lights. They all want different shaped lanterns.

I like the pyramid shaped lanterns best.

I prefer the cube shapes.

Sphere shapes for me.

Let's get a third of each, then everyone will be happy!

1. How many pyramid-shaped lanterns are there? They buy a third of these. How many will they buy?

2. How many cube-shaped lanterns are there? They buy a third of these. How many will they buy?

3. How many sphere-shaped lanterns are there? They buy a third of these. How many will they buy? How many lanterns will they buy altogether?

12. Yum Yum Chocolate Cake

Objective

◉ Recognise fractions which are equivalent to one and pairs of fractions that add up to one

---

Resources

◉ Four small circles cut from paper for each child

Introduction

◉ Do children like chocolate cake? You could draw a Carroll diagram with the headings 'chocolate cake/not chocolate cake' and ask children to add their names.

◉ Agree that the cake has been cut into slices. What fraction could be used to describe one slice? Establish this would be $\frac{1}{8}$, one of the 8 slices. Ask children to tell you all they know about fractions.

◉ Draw 4 rectangles of the same size on the board. Label the first '1'. Divide the second in half. Ask children what fraction you have made. Label each with '$\frac{1}{2}$'. Ask them to write an addition sentence to show that two halves make a whole. Repeat this for the next two rectangles which you divide into quarters and eighths. Ask children to identify any equivalent fractions, e.g. $\frac{2}{4} = \frac{1}{2}$, $\frac{2}{8} = \frac{1}{4}$, $\frac{3}{4} = \frac{1}{2} + \frac{1}{4}$.

Solutions

1. $\frac{1}{8}$, $\frac{7}{8}$

2. $\frac{2}{8}$, $\frac{1}{4}$

3. $\frac{6}{8}$, $\frac{3}{4}$. No, there will only be 6 slices left and there are 7 toys.

During the activity

1. How many eighths make up a whole? Agree 8. Next ask children to make up an addition sentence to show this ($\frac{1}{8} + \frac{1}{8} + \frac{1}{8} + \frac{1}{8} + \frac{1}{8} + \frac{1}{8} + \frac{1}{8} + \frac{1}{8} = 1$). Discuss ways of making one in different ways using eighths, e.g. $\frac{1}{8} + \frac{7}{8} = 1$. How many ways can they find?

2. Give each child four small circles and ask them to pretend these are cakes. What ways can they find to divide them into equal slices?

3. Suggest they make one of the circles look like the cake in the picture and use this to help them answer the questions.

4. For question 1, ask children to write an addition sentence to show that the two fractions make a whole, e.g. $\frac{1}{8} + \frac{7}{8} = 1$. For question 2, they write an addition and a subtraction sentence to show their answer, e.g. $\frac{1}{8} + \frac{1}{8} = \frac{2}{8}$, $1 - \frac{2}{8} = \frac{6}{8}$.

Extension

1. Ask children to write down some equivalent fractions, starting with those discussed in the main activity, e.g. $\frac{1}{2} = \frac{2}{4} = \frac{4}{8}$. Can they see a pattern? Establish that for each of these they double the numerator and the denominator. Ask them to write another five fractions that are equivalent to these.

2. Write some unit fractions on the board, e.g. $\frac{1}{4}$, $\frac{1}{2}$, $\frac{1}{5}$, $\frac{1}{10}$, $\frac{1}{3}$. Children make up fraction addition sentences to show how many of these total one, e.g. $\frac{1}{2} + \frac{2}{4} = 1$.

Maths words

fraction, numerator, denominator, equivalent fraction, unit fraction

Yum Yum Chocolate Cake

Sophie is sharing her cake with her toys.

1. Sophie eats one slice of cake. What fraction of the cake is this? What fraction will be left?

2. Sophie wants to eat 2 slices of cake. What fraction of the cake is this? Write your answer using two different fractions.

3. What fraction will be left if Sophie eats two slices? Write your answer using two different fractions. Will her toys each be able to have a slice if she eats two? How do you know this?

13. Birthday Presents

Objective

- Make 2D and 3D shapes, recognise in different orientations, and describe with increasing accuracy

Resources

- Plasticine® or similar
- Cubes, cuboids, card, scissors and sticky tape for extension activity

Introduction

- Can children tell you what the 3D shapes in the picture are? Discuss the properties of each in terms of number of faces, edges and vertices. Stress that faces are flat surfaces, edges are where faces meet and vertices are where edges meet. Inform children that spheres, cylinders and cones have curved surfaces and that the cone has an apex.

- Children make a poster together to show the properties of these 3D shapes.

During the activity

1. Give each child a piece of plasticine. Ask them to identify the sphere in the picture and then make their plasticine into one. They describe its properties, talk about what it can do (i.e. roll) and what they might see in the real world that looks like this.

Solutions

1. Sphere (1 curved surface, 0 vertices, 0 edges); cylinder (1 curved surface, 2 faces, 0 vertices, 2 edges); cone (1 curved surface, 1 face, 0 vertices, 1 apex, 1 edge); small cube, larger cube, cuboid (all have 6 faces, 8 vertices, 12 edges); square-based pyramid (5 faces, 5 vertices, 8 edges); triangular prism (5 faces, 6 vertices, 9 edges)

2. Square, rectangle, triangle, circle

3. Check children's answers.

2. Do the same for the cube. Discuss what they did (i.e. flatten the curves to make flat surfaces) and talk about its properties, including the shapes of its faces and what things in real life are this shape. Repeat for the cuboid, noting whether the number of faces, edges and vertices have changed and what is now different.

3. Talk about 2D shapes. Children identify these shapes in the classroom.

Extension

1. Children make a square-based pyramid from plasticine. Ask them to visualise what it would look like if the triangular faces were pulled down (i.e. a square with a triangle attached to each of its sides). They sketch this on paper, cut it out and make the pyramid. Discuss how their pyramid could become more accurate. Establish that they could measure the square and also make the triangles the same size. Give them the opportunity to make an accurate net and pyramid.

2. Give each child a cube or cuboid, card, scissors and sticky tape. Ask them to look very carefully at their shape and to make it with the card. Do any draw a net or the beginnings of one?

3. Children make a cube out of plasticine and then create its net. They could explore nets of the other shapes with faces from the picture.

Maths words

3D shapes, 2D shapes, face, vertex, edge, side, corner, all shape names

Birthday Presents

It's Sam's birthday. He has lots of presents! They are all different shapes. What could they be?

1. Write down the 3D shape names of each present. Write the number of curved surfaces, faces, vertices and edges each has.

2. Now draw all the different shaped faces of the presents. Label these with their 2D shape names.

3. What do you think could be in Sam's presents? Write an idea for each shape and say why you think this.

14. Worms, Worms, Worms

Objectives

◉ Recognise and use full names and abbreviations for metric units of measure

◉ Measure, compare, add and subtract: lengths (m/cm/mm)

Resources

◉ Plasticine® or similar

◉ String and rulers

Introduction

◉ Ask children about the picture. Discuss what a wormery is.

◉ Ask children to tell you what can be measured, e.g. how heavy something is (mass), how much something holds (capacity), how long something is (length), how hot or cold something is (temperature).

◉ Ask children to tell you all the units that they use to measure length. Ensure they include millimetres, centimetres, metres and kilometres. Some may say miles, feet and inches. Explain that metric and imperial are two types of measurement. Imperial units were introduced by the British and used by countries that were part of the British Empire. In the late 20th century many began using metric measurements, but some still use imperial measurements. Others, e.g. UK, use a mixture.

◉ Focus on metric units. Ask children to make an information poster by writing these in words with their abbreviation, e.g. millimetre mm. Then they add the equivalences between millimetre and centimetre, centimetre and metre to their poster. They could decorate it with appropriate pictures.

During the activity

1. Establish that children need to measure the two worms that have escaped from the jar. Discuss the units that might be used to measure their length.

2. Give each child some plasticine. Ask them to roll it into the longest worm they can in 30 seconds. In a group of four, they order their worms from shortest to longest. They then estimate the length of the shortest and measure it. They use this measurement to estimate the length of the second shortest, continuing until they have estimated and measured the length of all the worms. Did their estimating improve? They then draw the lengths of their worms on paper and label them.

Extension

1. Ask children to measure the lengths of five different items in the classroom. They convert their measurement to another unit and record both.

2. Children find the differences between pairs of the lengths.

Solutions

1. Children's estimates
2. Approximately 7 cm, 70 mm; 4 cm, 40 mm
3. 3 cm, 30 mm

Maths words

length, measure, unit, centimetre, millimetre, equivalent

Worms, Worms, Worms

These children have found some worms in their garden. They want to find out how long two of them are.

1. How many worms can you see? Why is it difficult to know exactly how many there are?

2. Look at the two worms. Estimate how long they are and draw them on a piece of paper. Give your answer in cm and then in mm.

3. How much longer is the long worm? Give your answer in cm and then in mm.

15. Fruit Salad

Objectives

🌀 Recognise and use full names and abbreviations for metric units of measure

🌀 Measure, compare, add and subtract: lengths (m/cm/mm); mass (kg/g); volume/capacity (l/ml)

Resources

🌀 Weighing scales, sand/rice, plastic food bags

🌀 Measuring jugs, bottles of water, containers

🌀 Rulers to draw number lines

Introduction

🌀 Ask children what they can see in the picture. Can they identify the fruit? You could ask them their favourite fruit, make a tally and discuss how the tally could be represented, e.g. as a pictogram.

🌀 Ask children what things can be weighed and what units would be suitable, e.g. a person in kilograms, a feather in grams.

🌀 Give small groups of children a set of scales, a container of sand/rice and some plastic bags. Ask them to estimate how much sand would weigh the same as each fruit in the recipe in the picture. They put what they think in a bag and then weigh it and label each bag with the amount.

During the activity

1. Ask children what types of measurement Millie will use, i.e. mass and capacity. Ask children what the abbreviations for the units in her recipe mean. Recall how many grams are in a kilogram. Ask questions, e.g. how many grams are in $\frac{1}{2}$ kg, 2.5 kg, 3 kg, etc?

2. Children list the weights in the recipe and then write them in other ways, e.g. bananas 0.7 kg, 700 g.

3. Discuss capacity as the amount a container will hold and volume as the amount of liquid that is inside a container. Ask what units are used to measure these and how many millilitres are in a litre. Give small groups a bottle of water and a container. They estimate the amount of orange juice Millie needs and put this into a container. Then they measure accurately using a measuring jug.

Extension

1. Ask children to make up some mixed units of mass, e.g. 3 kg 450 g. They then write these in two other ways, e.g. 3450 g and 3.45 kg. They plot them on a number line and find the difference between pairs of their weights.

2. Repeat for units of capacity, e.g. 2 l 125 ml: 2125 ml, 2.125 l.

Solutions

1. 400 g, 500 g, 700 g, 800 g. Difference: 400 g

2. Banana 1400 g (1 kg 400 g, 1.4 kg), kiwi 800 g (0.8 kg), apple 1600 g (1 kg 600 g, 1.6 kg), peach 1000 g (1 kg), orange juice 1000 ml (1 l)

3. 4800 g or 4 kg 800 g or 4.8 kg

Maths words

mass, weigh, gram, kilogram, capacity, measuring jug, millilitre, litre

Fruit Salad

Millie's friends are coming for tea. She is making fruit salad for them.

1. Order the weights of the fruits from lightest to heaviest. Draw a number line from 0 to 1 kg and plot these amounts onto it. What is the difference between the lightest and heaviest amounts?

2. Millie's recipe is for 6 people. Write the recipe to feed 12 people.

3. Work out the total weight of fruit that Millie needs. Write the total in g and then kg and g.

16. The Farmer's Fence

Objective

⟳ Measure the perimeter of simple 2D shapes

Resources

⟳ Centimetre-squared paper

⟳ Plain paper, rulers

Introduction

⟳ Ask children what the farmer needs help with. He needs to find out how much it will cost to put a fence around his sheep field. Ask children what the outside of an area like the field is called. Establish that it is a perimeter which, as it is a length, is measured in millimetres, centimetres, metres and kilometres.

⟳ Ask children which things in the classroom have a perimeter and to give an appropriate unit, e.g. the perimeter of the whiteboard would be in metres.

During the activity

1. Each child draws a square following the lines on a piece of squared paper. They find its perimeter. Take feedback on how they did this. Did they count the centimetre lines around the outside one at a time or did they use a more efficient method? Discuss that, as a square has sides of equal length, they could count one side and multiply by 4 by doubling and doubling again. They draw some more squares and find their perimeters using this method.

2. Next explore perimeters of rectangles. Children draw one on squared paper and think about an efficient way to add the lengths of sides, e.g. double the length of the longer side and add this to double the length of the shorter side. Ask them to do this for several rectangles. They can now work out the perimeter of the field (tell them to ignore the length of the gate if anyone asks).

3. Discuss using addition or multiplication to find out the cost of the fencing.

Extension

1. Ask children to draw different squares and rectangles on plain paper. They use rulers to measure the sides and use an efficient method to find the perimeters.

2. Using centimetre-squared paper, children investigate all the rectangles they can draw with a perimeter of 24 cm. Can they find all six (or 11 if they draw the five pairs that use the same lengths in different orientations)? Ask them to look at the pattern and tell you what is happening.

3. Children draw a simple compound shape on their squared paper and work out the perimeter.

Maths words

perimeter, distance, millimetre, centimetre, metre, kilometre

Solutions

1. 240 m

2. £2400

3. £200; £2600

The Farmer's Fence

The farmer needs a new fence around his field to keep his sheep safe.

1. What is the perimeter of the farmer's field? Show how you worked this out.

2. How much will it cost him to buy enough fencing to go all the way around the field? Show how you worked this out.

3. The farmer also wants to buy two gates. How much will they cost? Add this to the cost of the fencing. How much is the total cost?

17. Feeding Time at the Zoo

Objective

🌀 Tell and write the time from an analogue clock, and 12-hour and 24-hour digital clocks

Resources

🌀 Clocks

🌀 Clock outlines

🌀 Rulers to draw time number lines

Introduction

🌀 What is the picture about? Have children ever been to a zoo? What was the best part of the visit? Did they see animals being fed?

🌀 Ask children to tell you all they know about time. Cover: analogue clocks, digital clocks, 12- and 24-hour time, a.m. and p.m., plus other vocabulary, e.g. yesterday, morning.

🌀 Give each child a clock. Call out times in both analogue and digital formats for them to find.

During the activity

1. Ask what sort of times the feeding times are. Establish that they are digital clock times.

2. Give children some problems relating to the picture, e.g. the children were watching the penguins being fed at 10:15, stayed there for 20 minutes and then took 10 minutes to walk to the emus. At what time did they arrive? Children follow this using their clocks and show you the final time.

Solutions

1. Quarter past 10, half past 11, quarter to 1, 2 o'clock, half past 2, quarter past 3

2. 5 hours

3. 1 hour 15 minutes, 1 hour 15 minutes, 1 hour 15 minutes, 30 minutes, 45 minutes. Yes.

3. Write the feeding times on the board. Draw a time number line. Ask children to choose two times. Place the earliest time at the beginning of the time number line and the latest at the end. Demonstrate how to find the difference between the two by counting on in hours and then minutes from the earliest to the latest, e.g. 12:45 + one hour is 1:45, plus 15 minutes is 2:00, plus 30 minutes is 2:30, so the difference is 1 hour and 45 minutes. They then find differences between other pairs of times.

4. Remind children to draw one hand longer than the other when drawing the times on their clock faces and to work out time differences on a time number line.

Extension

1. Give children more outline clocks. Working with a partner, they take turns to give each other times within the context of the picture, e.g. they went to the café at 5 minutes past 2. They draw the times on their clocks and label them with the digital equivalent.

2. Give children eight times to convert to 12-hour digital times using a.m. or p.m. Then they write these as 24-hour times and plot these on a time number line. They find the differences between pairs of them.

3. Children make up some time problems related to the picture to ask the class.

Maths words

time, analogue, digital, hour, minute, o'clock, quarter past/to, half past

Feeding Time at the Zoo

The children are visiting the zoo. They would like to see all the animals being fed.

1. Draw the feeding times on clock faces and label them with their analogue times.

2. What is the difference between the earliest and latest feeding times?

3. Work out how long it is between feeding times. They need 30 minutes between the times to see all the animals being fed. Can they get to each one in time?

18. On the Buses

Objective

◎ Compare durations of events, e.g. to calculate the time taken up by particular events or tasks

Resources

◎ Paper printed with 9 outline clock faces, without hands

◎ Rulers to draw time number lines

◎ Clocks

Introduction

◎ Ask children to tell you what they think is happening in the picture. Agree it is a family waiting for a bus to take them to the cinema and they are wondering if they will get there in time.

◎ You could ask children if they ever go to the cinema and what their favourite films are.

◎ Focus on the timetable and discuss what types of time it shows. Agree that these are 24-hour clock times. Where have children seen these sorts of times? Discuss the fact that they are found on travel timetables. They are also seen on clocks, computers, phones, etc.

During the activity

1. Give children a copy of the clock face outlines. Ask them to convert the 24-hour clock times on the bus timetable to analogue times and draw these on the clock faces.

2. Children should use time number lines for this task. Together work out how long it takes for each bus to travel from Dendridge to Portland, e.g. for the 270 bus, place 15:45 at the beginning of their time number lines, add 15 minutes to get to 16:00 hours and place this in the middle of their timeline and then add 15 minutes to get to 16:15 and place this at the end of their timeline. They then add the two 15 minutes to make 30 minutes.

Extension

1. Tell children that the buses are all running 25 minutes late. Ask them when each bus will arrive at its destination.

2. Give children a selection of 24-hour clock times, e.g. 08:17, 10:35, 13:02, 18:45. Ask them to find the differences between them. Remind them to use time number lines.

3. Ask children to make up their own bus timetable for two buses. They could use locations they are familiar with. They then work out journey times from one place to another.

Maths words

time, analogue, digital, 24-hour time, fastest, slowest

Solutions

1. 270 (fastest bus): 15 minutes, 319: 25 minutes, 480: 30 minutes

2. 270: 45 minutes, 319: 1 hour, 480 (slowest bus): 1 hour 15 minutes

3. Yes because the bus arrives at 5:15, the film starts at 5:30 and the bus stop is really close to the cinema.

On the Buses

Katie and her family are going to the cinema in Portland. She is worried they might miss the film.

Luckily the cinema is really close to the Portland bus stop.

1. How long does it take each bus to travel from Sunbury to Dendridge? Which is the fastest bus?

2. How long does it take each bus to travel from Sunbury to Portland? Which is the slowest bus?

3. Will Katie and her family get to the cinema in time to see the film? Explain how you know this.

19. School Dinners

Objectives

⊚ Read, interpret and present data using pictograms with scales

⊚ Solve problems using information presented in pictograms and tables

Resources

⊚ Plain paper, rulers

Introduction

⊚ Ask children to tell you what they can see in the picture. Agree it shows children eating their school dinner which they don't like and that there is a pictogram showing what they would prefer to eat.

⊚ What can children tell you about pictograms?

⊚ Invite volunteers to read what the children are saying in the speech bubbles. Do they know or can they guess what a survey is and what a vote is? Ask the class which of these foods they would choose for their school dinners.

During the activity

1. Discuss the number of children each symbol and half symbol represents.

2. Ask children to work with a partner to make a list of six pieces of information that the pictogram tells them. Encourage them to include statements that involve addition and subtraction, e.g. 3 more children prefer roast dinner than casserole, 55 children took part in the survey, 13 children voted for vegetable lasagne and chicken pie. They share these with another pair, adding any new statements to their list.

3. Remind children to give their tables column headings and a title of their choice.

Extension

1. Children use the information in the pictogram to make a bar chart. The vertical axis should go up in intervals of 2.

2. Ask children to make a survey of the class' favourite meals. They select six of them and then ask everyone for their preferred choice. They do this as a tally. They then make this into a pictogram to show the information. They could then make statements from their pictogram to share with the rest of the class.

Maths words

table, pictogram, symbol, survey, vote

Solutions

1. Vegetable lasagne; 4

2.

School dinner	Number of votes
Roast dinner	16
Casserole	13
Chicken pie	9
Cottage pie	7
Cheese salad	6
Vegetable lasagne	4

3. Chicken pie, casserole and roast dinner because more children voted for these.

School Dinners

The children are fed up with their school dinners. They have carried out a survey to show what food they really want.

1. What is the least popular meal? How many children voted for it?

2. Turn the pictogram into a table and write the numbers of children who like the different meal choices.

3. What three meals do the children think the cook should make? Explain how you know this.

20. Vegetables

Objective

⊚ Solve problems using information presented in pictograms and tables

Resources

⊚ Plain paper, rulers

Introduction

⊚ Ask children to tell you what they can see in the picture. Agree Mrs Yam needs help deciding which vegetables to sell. Can children identify the vegetables? Do they eat these? You could do a survey of the vegetables that they like, making a tally and then a table to show this.

⊚ Invite volunteers to tell everyone what they know about bar graphs. Draw out the fact that the intervals go up in 2s. Discuss other ways this information could be represented, e.g. table, pictogram.

During the activity

1. Encourage children to use a ruler to find the height of each bar in the picture, by placing it across the top of each bar and lining it up with the vertical axis.

2. Ask children to turn the information on the bar chart in the picture into a pictogram. They should choose their own symbol and make it represent 2 people. They could then ask the rest of the class which of the vegetables in the picture that they would choose and add this to their pictogram. Ask them to make statements from it that involve addition and subtraction.

3. Ask children to find out the favourite vegetables of the class. They should record this as a tally. They could then make a table. Once they have their table they then use this to make up eight questions that they can ask the rest of the class, e.g. which vegetables are more popular than x, how many more children like y than z?

Extension

1. Using the information collected in activity 3 above and from the picture, children make a bar graph to show the data. If any vegetable choices are the same as in the picture, they need to combine the votes. Expect them to choose a suitable scale for the vertical axis.

Maths words

data, tally, table, bar graph, survey, vote

Solutions

1. Sprouts because only 11 people voted for them.

2. Spinach 26, sweet corn 25

3.

Vegetable	Number of votes
Spinach	26
Sweet corn	25
Potatoes	24
Carrots	22
Leeks	20
Cabbage	17

Vegetables

Mrs Yam is a greengrocer. She wants to sell the vegetables that her customers like.

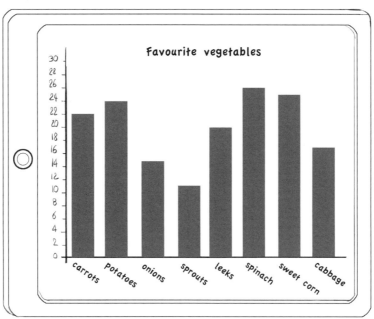

I can't decide which six vegetables to sell.

1. Which is the least popular vegetable? How do you know?

2. Which are the two most popular vegetables? How many people voted for them?

3. Draw a table to show the six vegetables that Mrs Yam should sell and how many people voted for each.

Random number cards

Give these number cards to children to make 2-, 3-, 4- and 5-digit numbers. For example, ask them to make 249, and then ask them to rearrange the digits to make as many new 3-digit numbers as they can.

2	3	4	5
6	7	8	9
1	2	3	4
5	6	7	8
0	4	3	1
6	8	9	0

Partitioning cards: ones, tens and hundreds

These cards can be used to demonstrate the construction and partitioning of 2- and 3-digit numbers. Children can partition and rearrange the numbers to secure their understanding of place value. For example, say 367. Children combine the 300, 60 and 7. Ask them to show you the tens number and say it. Repeat for the hundreds and ones.

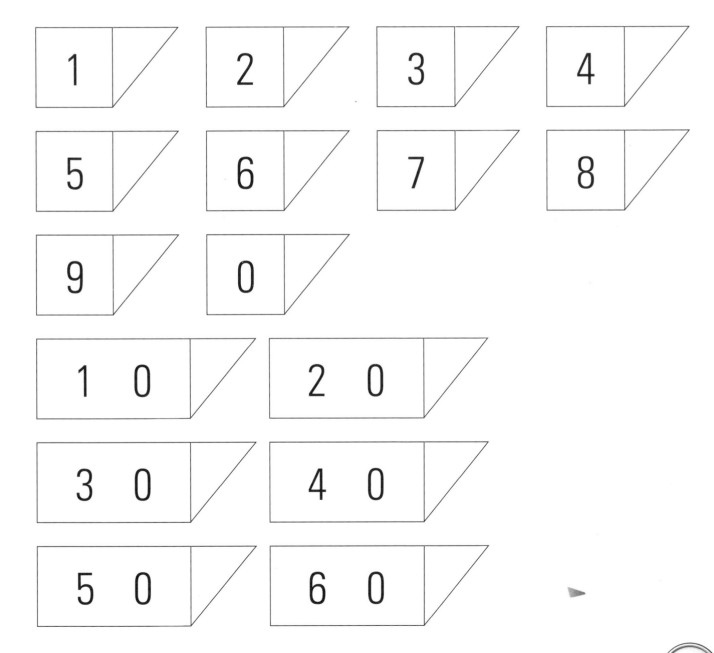

7 0	8 0
9 0	0 0
1 0 0	2 0 0
3 0 0	4 0 0
5 0 0	6 0 0
7 0 0	8 0 0
9 0 0	0 0 0

Time matching cards

Cut out these cards. Children can use them to play snap or a matching game.

4:45	5:15	6:00	7:30
2:05	7:45	11:50	3:15
quarter to five	quarter past five	six o'clock	half past seven
twenty minutes to four o'clock	five minutes to two o'clock	ten minutes past ten o'clock	twenty-five minutes to one o'clock

47

Glossary

[activity number]

24-hour time [18]
2D/3D shapes [13]

add [3, 4, 5, 6]
addition [3, 4, 5]
altogether [3]
analogue [17, 18]
array [10]

bar graph [20]

capacity [15]
centimetre (cm) [14, 16]
corner [13]
count in 2s, 5s [2]

data [20]
denominator [11, 12]
difference [1, 4, 5]
digital [17, 18]
digits [1]
distance [16]
divide [6, 7, 9, 10]
division [7, 9]
divisor [9]
double [7, 8]

edge [13]
equal [10]
equivalent [14]
equivalent fraction [12]
estimate [1, 3]

face [13]
fastest [18]
fraction [11, 12]

gram (g) [15]
groups of [9]

half past [17]
halve [8]
hour [17]
how much more/less [5]
hundreds [1, 2]

inverse operation [6]

kilogram (kg) [15]
kilometre (km) [16]

length [14]
litre [15]

mass [15]
measure [14]
measuring jug [15]
metre [16]
minute [17]
missing number [6]
millilitre (ml) [15]
millimetre (mm) [14, 16]
more [3]
multiple [2]
multiplication [7, 8]
multiply [6, 7, 8, 10]

numerals [1]
numerator [11, 12]

o'clock [17]
ones [1, 2]
order [2]

partition [1, 8]
perimeter [16]
pictogram [19]
place value [1]

quarter past/to [17]

shape names [13]
side [13]
slowest [18]
subtract [4, 5, 6]
survey [19, 20]
symbol [19]

table [19, 20]
take away [4, 5]
tally [20]
tens [1, 2]
time [17, 18]
times [8]
total [1, 3, 4, 5, 10]

unit [14]
unit fraction [11, 12]

vertex [13]
vote [19, 20]

weigh [15]